D0434830

Queen for a Day

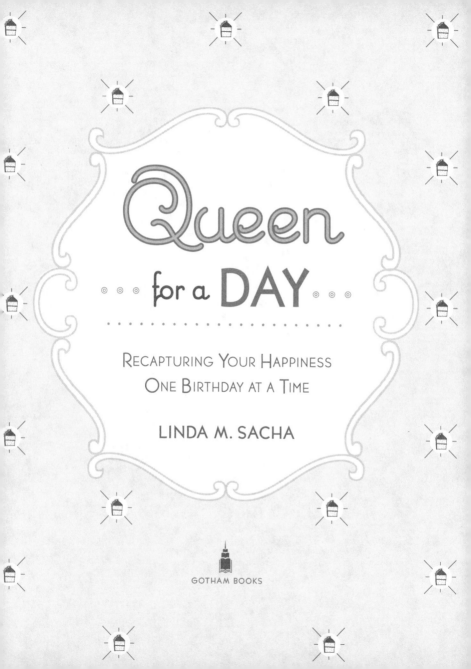

Queen
··· for a DAY ···

RECAPTURING YOUR HAPPINESS
ONE BIRTHDAY AT A TIME

LINDA M. SACHA

GOTHAM BOOKS

GOTHAM BOOKS
PUBLISHED BY PENGUIN GROUP (USA) INC.
375 HUDSON STREET, NEW YORK, NEW YORK 10014, U.S.A.
PENGUIN GROUP (CANADA), 90 EGLINTON AVENUE EAST, SUITE 700, TORONTO, ONTARIO M4P 2Y3, CANADA (A DIVISION OF PEARSON PENGUIN CANADA INC.); PENGUIN BOOKS LTD, 80 STRAND, LONDON WC2R 0RL, ENGLAND; PENGUIN IRELAND, 25 ST STEPHEN'S GREEN, DUBLIN 2, IRELAND (A DIVISION OF PENGUIN BOOKS LTD); PENGUIN GROUP (AUSTRALIA), 250 CAMBERWELL ROAD, CAMBERWELL, VICTORIA 3124, AUSTRALIA (A DIVISION OF PEARSON AUSTRALIA GROUP PTY LTD); PENGUIN BOOKS INDIA PVT LTD, 11 COMMUNITY CENTRE, PANCHSHEEL PARK, NEW DELHI—110 017, INDIA; PENGUIN GROUP (NZ), 67 APOLLO DRIVE, ROSEDALE, NORTH SHORE 0632, NEW ZEALAND (A DIVISION OF PEARSON NEW ZEALAND LTD); PENGUIN BOOKS (SOUTH AFRICA) (PTY) LTD, 24 STURDEE AVENUE, ROSEBANK, JOHANNESBURG 2196, SOUTH AFRICA

PENGUIN BOOKS LTD, REGISTERED OFFICES: 80 STRAND, LONDON WC2R 0RL, ENGLAND

PUBLISHED BY GOTHAM BOOKS, A MEMBER OF PENGUIN GROUP (USA) INC.

FIRST PRINTING, DECEMBER 2009
10 9 8 7 6 5 4 3 2 1

LIBRARY OF CONGRESS CATALOGING-IN-PUBLICATION DATA
SACHA, LINDA M.
  QUEEN FOR A DAY: RECAPTURING YOUR HAPPINESS ONE BIRTHDAY AT A TIME / LINDA M. SACHA.
    P. CM.
  ISBN 978-1-59240-527-5 (PBK.)
  1. BIRTHDAYS. I. TITLE.
  GT2430.S23 2009
  394.2—DC22
                                                    2009024814
PRINTED IN THE UNITED STATES OF AMERICA
SET IN CAECILIA BOLD
BOOK DESIGN BY SUSAN HOOD

THIS BOOK IS DEDICATED TO MY MOM, Donna;

AND MY AUNTS Pat, Maryanne, Carol,

Charlotte, Della, AND Mary.

YOU ALWAYS MADE US FEEL LIKE OUR BIRTHDAYS

WERE YOUR GREATEST PRIORITY.

AND TO Linda Marie, MY BIRTHDAY CHAMPION.

I LOVE YOU ALL, ALWAYS.

CONTENTS

Queen for a Day

··· an ···

Invitation

YOU ARE HOLDING a special book. It's about you and me and women everywhere. It's about birthdays. It's an invitation to get in touch with your heart's true desires and celebrate yourself like never before.

How did you get this book? Perhaps you bought it for yourself because you already love your birthday and want to record your memories. Maybe it was a gift from a friend who hopes you will take greater pleasure in your special day. Whatever the reason, I'm glad you're here. Welcome to the journey of recapturing your birthday joy.

I began this project because I wanted to create a way for women to use their birthdays as an opportunity for reflection and growth, as well as celebration. Your birthday is a powerful day to examine where you are, where you want to go, and how you can manifest your dreams—it's a personal anniversary that can serve as a springboard for shaping the rest of your life. My mission is to help women around the world to know, love, and trust themselves more, beginning with their birthdays.

Each year I keep a birthday journal, and fill it with my own answers to the questions you'll find in this book. If someone had given me a birthday journal a few years ago, I would have thought, "Oh, that's nice," and promptly tossed it in a drawer. There was a process of self-discovery that led to my establishing this precious birthday ritual. So, in addition to the journal pages, I'd like to share with you the journey of becoming a Birthday Queen—a woman who has learned to cherish her day of birth—and the steps and inspiration that will enable you to look forward to celebrating yourself each year. In the years that follow, I hope you will continue to use your special day as an opportunity for renewal by keeping a personal birthday journal of your own, long after the pages of this book are filled.

Through years of disappointment, compromise, and growth, my birthday has evolved into an exceptional event. Along the way I wondered whether I was alone in my struggles and joy. I made it my mission to find out how other women felt about their birthdays. Through a global survey and countless conversations, I gathered secret birthday thoughts. I found some women who adored their birthdays and others, like me, who had been treating their day of birth as a second-class holiday. Less than half of the women surveyed considered their birthdays "very important" and only one third were satisfied

 with how their day went. Though I discovered many different attitudes, I learned that birthdays are a universally hot topic—it's a day we love to love or love to hate. These women, too, inspired me to create this book, and you'll find their insightful quotes throughout.

On my birthday I normally celebrate quietly with my family and thank my mother for the gift of life.

—Patty R.
age 51

I just love my birthday! I always think of that day as a new starting place, and get excited wondering what new happenings are in store for me.

—KATHY A., AGE 50

Birthdays don't matter very much to me, although they probably should since it's the day I entered the world. I'm neither pleased nor displeased because it's just another day to me.

—SANDY R., AGE 58

As I shared my journey with family and friends, an amazing thing happened: One by one, each woman embarked on her own personal quest, discovering her heart's unique desires and learning to relish the day on which she was born. I invite you to explore and expand on the idea of creating a day that's filled with what and who you love. It is a journey for all women who choose to love themselves as much as they love others—at least one day of the year. It is an invitation to reclaim your crown.

Childhood Birthday Joy

I AM A PROFESSIONAL, mature, fairly sane woman who found that on many of my adult birthdays, I would turn into an immature, somewhat irrational, disappointed child. My secret expectations for my gloriously special day were often unmet. I had slowly but surely shut down my birthday joy and muttered things like, "Oh, what's the big deal—it's just another day." Secretly, I was denying myself one of my sweetest desires—to be fussed over one day of the year.

When I was growing up, birthdays at our house were a BIG deal—or I should say they felt

My childhood experiences of birthdays have
a lot to do with how I feel about them now—
they are charmed or special days when I am
entitled to a bit more positive attention.

—Kathleen D.

age 47

like a big deal to me at the time, and that's all that mattered. My dad would wake me up singing "Happy Birthday" and ask me how I wanted my eggs. The night before, my mom would bake gooey treats for me to share at school. Classmates would stuff their faces and treat me like their best friend. The nuns would pin a special badge on my uniform, so that everyone smiled adoringly at me, and the cafeteria lady would give me an extra cling peach. I would arrive home to find my favorite dinner being prepared, and that evening family members would stream into the house to sing, eat cake, and bestow a present or two.

By the time I collapsed into bed it was crystal clear that I was a Birthday Princess. I felt special—and it wasn't about gifts. Some years, dinner was Spam,

Sometimes I get a huge goodie, other times we do dinner and a card. What I care about most is his fuss over me. Any gift is an extra.

—Mary Jane S.,
age 75

the present was a coloring book or pajamas I needed anyway, and the entertainment was a talent show starring my cousins and me. Truly, fancy food, expensive gifts, and dazzling entertainment were not the focus. I was. It was all about basking in the recognition that today was my day. I was born—and that was worth celebrating.

Hitting Birthday Bottom

FLASH FORWARD twenty years or so to adulthood. Family and friends working ten-hour days, life moving at a techno-frantic pace—not a cupcake in sight. My husband arrives home and lovingly hands me flowers. "Happy birthday, honey."

Hmmm. He remembered my birthday. Flowers are nice. This ought to be enough. Without fully understanding why, I slip into the birthday doldrums. "What's the big deal," I repeat to myself. After all, birthdays are for kids.

Then I hit birthday bottom.

My husband was working out of town, I had just started a new job, and none of my coworkers knew it was my birthday. My parents and sisters were on vacation and most of my friends just plain forgot. I never said a word. Isn't that what adults are supposed to do? As the day progressed, I felt myself slumping deeper into sadness. Oh, just grow up and get over this birthday stuff—it's darn selfish to expect a lot of attention.

I cried all the way home from work.

Questions raced through my mind: How come no one made my breakfast? Why isn't someone baking a cake? Isn't anyone going to sing a little birthday song to me? Didn't I feel like a princess just a decade or two ago? Where the heck is my extra cling peach? How exactly did this happen? I love my birthday and I want it back!

Long gone were the days of the Super 8 and loving parents taking charge of making me feel like a birthday superstar. Now it was up to me, and I was feeling pretty mopey about the whole thing.

—KAREN G., AGE 39

When we're children, most of us don't have to plan our own birthday. Our parents remember, teachers have it in their file, grandmas have it permanently burned in their brain. We just filled in the blanks as grown-ups initiated the questions: "What color icing would you like? Who would you like to have sleep over? Would you like hot dogs or macaroni and cheese?" If we don't have someone asking us these questions, how easy it is to slip into a mode of noncelebration. The little girl in me still had the same desires and expectations—I just didn't understand that I was now in charge.

I got married, moved away from my family, and unconsciously assumed my husband would take over as birthday coordinator. This was the beginning of my birthday demise. Is my partner adorable, wonderful, and loving? Yep. Did he get the birthday routine? Nope. Did I think he should have read my mind and psychically divined my secret desires? Yessiree. Did I pout, act hurt, and say I didn't care for many years? Uh-huh. Slowly, reality set in: Why should he know about this birthday stuff? He was raised in an all-boy family that didn't make a big fuss over birthdays, and he dislikes being the center of attention. Was it possible that I was in charge of my own birthday happiness, and it was my responsibility to ask for what I want?

Darn. This is going to take some effort on my part, isn't it?

Reclaiming
My Crown

WHEN I REALIZED that I was in charge, it took me time to learn *how* to create it for myself. I remained captive to common birthday thoughts like, "I just don't have time to make my day special" or "I can't afford to spend money on myself right now." In the words of my therapist friends, Jim and Sari: "If you hear yourself using an excuse that involves time or money, then you haven't gotten to the real reason—there's something else."

I eventually realized that when a woman ignores her birthday, it signals a deeper issue involving commitment,

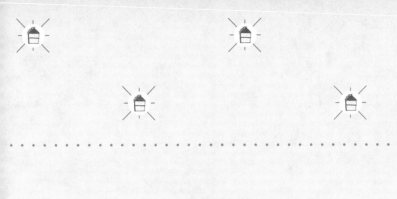

Thank you, Mother, thank you, Daddy. Thanks to my ancestors who came before me. I am here today because of you and I am eternally grateful for the best gift of all—the gift of life.

—Linda M.

age 59

priorities, and most of all, self-love. Acknowledging one's birthday is an act of recognizing that you are worth celebrating. After much introspection and growth, the result was, and continues to be, the official rebirth of a grown-up Birthday Princess—the Birthday Queen. A woman who deserves the same happiness that we experienced as children and one who takes pleasure in making it happen. It's a journey that you will experience in the section called "Five Steps to Reclaiming Your Crown."

Of course, it didn't all magically happen at once. I tiptoed the first year and told my husband what I'd "kind of" like as a gift. I bravely dove in my second year and told everyone, "Tomorrow is my birthday—don't forget to sing!" And five years later for my big 4-0, I threw myself a party in which the guests came dressed as someone famous they'd like to be. I then coasted nicely into "birthday week," saying to my buddies, "My birthday's next month and I'd love to celebrate with you. Want to go to the movies? Let's walk on Tuesday. I've got time for the park on Thursday after work."

Nowadays, if you call our house

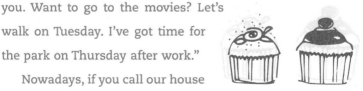

on my birthday you'll hear, "Hello, Birthday Headquarters!" My friends and family know how much I cherish my birthday, and just like when I was a child, it's not about presents. It's about feeling elated, loved, and in charge of my own happiness. Not a bad present, right?

Icing on the Cake

AS I REFLECT ON my journey, I find that as I have celebrated myself more, it has offered others the invitation to celebrate themselves more. There's a whole lot of crown swapping and plain old happiness going around these days.

The icing on the cake is that my husband now lives with a woman who is happy with herself and her birthday. I no longer act like an unhappy and confused child. I am a partner who cocreates my day with him. After he read this manuscript he looked up with tears in his eyes and said, "I get it. I really had no idea."

In that moment I knew I had possessed the crown all along and all I had to do was reclaim it for myself from myself.

I recently celebrated my fiftieth birthday. It was downright spectacular. Several months before, I sat down and really thought about how I wanted to honor this milestone in my life. I arranged private time with my husband and major girl time with my sisters. I spent time alone writing to four mentors, thanking them for the tremendous contributions they made to my life. I planned a celebration with friends and family and asked everyone to bring a favorite food. We danced in the living room as my friends' band played my favorite songs. I also fulfilled a lifelong fantasy of singing with a band. I belted out "Man! I Feel Like a Woman!" by Shania Twain and grinned through the entire song. Each woman at the party, as well as my girlfriends who weren't there, received a homemade present and a letter of appreciation for being an amazing woman.

At the end of it all I sat down and grinned from ear to ear. Someone commented that I had gone to a lot of trouble and asked if I minded putting together

We, as women, are hardwired to serve.
I began to seriously review my life—
everything I did was for someone else. I
didn't count. My friends and I organized
a Birthday Club and I had my first
birthday party when I was seventy-six.
We learned that we functioned much better
replenished than when we ran on fumes.

—Mary S.

age 79

my own celebration. It was so easy to reply, "I loved every second of planning and creating my happiness." In the last twenty years I had slowly but surely reclaimed my happiness one birthday at a time.

Once you're really immersed in your heart's desires, you begin to realize how good it feels—it's downright addictive—and when you're not honoring your true wants and needs, there's a void. Choosing and fulfilling your heart's desires one day of the year is great, two is even better, and then gradually, there are moments of greater self-love flowing into each day.

Susie, my dear friend of thirty-five  years, recently visited. I was thrilled to see her because she has a very busy life that includes a husband, three children, and pursuit of another degree. "You know I'm here as part of my monthly birthday adventure," she explained. I was confused because her birthday was six months ago. "Ever since you got me into this birthday stuff, I've found out how great it feels to take care of me occasionally. Since my fiftieth birthday, I plan something special every month that is just for my personal pleasure and claim it as my own."

Your Journey

RIGHT ABOUT NOW, you may be having one of several reactions to this whole Queen for a Day idea. Perhaps when you were growing up birthdays weren't a big deal or you don't have happy memories, so you may be having trouble relating to the idea that birthdays can actually be joyous or special. Maybe you're so busy being a wonder wife, partner, mom, executive, daughter, and more that you don't know where to begin. Or you may be saying, "What's all the fuss? I've always had great birthdays!"

I've always tried not to make a big deal out of my birthday since there wasn't much family around—that way you don't get disappointed. Last year my friends threw me a party. . . . I even got a pin that told everyone I was a Birthday Princess. And of course, a crown. It was the best birthday I've had in a very long time.

—Deborah P.

age 59

Here's the bottom line: Take a step forward from wherever you are . . .

Recapture it—if your birthdays used to be fun but recently they've been slipping away.

Refine it—if your birthdays have been acceptable but you'd love them to be even more fulfilling.

Re-create it—if you've never had a great birthday, because now is the time to make it so.

Rejoice in it—if you've been a birthday queen all along and it feels great to be validated for fully enjoying your day.

Queen for a Day
Credo

I AM A WOMAN
who loves myself enough to . . .

BELIEVE *that the day I came into this world is*
a day worth celebrating.

STOP AND THINK, *"What do I really want on my special day?"*

TAKE AT LEAST ONE DAY *of the year and completely*
immerse myself in my heart's desires.

KNOW that whining gets old and gets me nowhere, and that self-creation gets me everywhere I want to go.

BE COURAGEOUS enough to put my fears and pride aside and ask for what I want.

REALIZE that friends and family love participating in my special plans, knowing I'm doing exactly what makes me happy.

KNOW that I have the "ability to respond" if my birthday is anything less than delicious.

CLOSE MY EYES at the end of my special day, smile, and think, "That was superb and I deserved it!"

FULLY EMBRACE that reclaiming my crown is the greatest gift of love I can give myself and the world.

PART 2

Five Steps
... to ...
Reclaiming
Your Crown

THE PROCESS OF taking a step from wherever you are begins by embracing these steps:

1. I want and deserve at least one special day a year: I'm worth it!
2. It will be a pleasure to explore my heart's desires.
3. I will act on my heart's desires and create a happy birth day for myself.
4. I accept responsibility for my birthday: I own it.
5. In an annual loving birthday ritual, I will capture my thoughts, feelings, and dreams.

STEP 1. I Want and Deserve at Least One Special Day a Year: I'm Worth It!

FOR MANY YEARS I was a corporate trainer. One of my favorite authors is Tom Peters, who wrote several best-selling books on personal and managerial excellence. Step One on the Queen for a Day journey is best explained by a Peters quote: "a blinding flash of the obvious." The decision to want and believe you deserve a great birthday is simultaneously huge and obvious. It truly is the key to your kingdom. It's a willingness to proclaim:

I WANT to celebrate myself one day of the year and OF
COURSE I deserve it.

That's the bottom line. I love myself enough to create my day exactly as I want it. I was privileged to be put on this earth today, and I am going to celebrate.

I was recently flying out of Florida and found myself seated next to a friendly woman named Connie. She told me she had been working and then had taken some time to herself. When I told her about my birthday project, she burst into tears. It turned out that her "time to herself" was an escape to a condominium to celebrate her birthday—alone.

She explained, "My birthdays as an adult have been so awful that I dread them every year. This year, I decided to take care of myself and it was a big step." Connie was relieved when I told her that she had begun her induction as a Birthday Queen. With immense courage she had taken the first and hardest step—deciding that she wanted and deserved a special day.

Whether you prefer to dance with a room full of people or be alone—the decision to be true to yourself on your birthday is all yours.

A THOUGHT

Enhancing your self-worth is not an overnight process—it is a lifelong commitment that begins with one new loving thought about yourself. You have heard all of my past birthday excuses. What thoughts have gotten in the way of your past celebrations? Take an honest assessment and put a check mark next to any that you've heard yourself say.

☐ I just let it slip away.

☐ I forget about it.

☐ I'm too tired.

☐ I don't feel like I have enough time.

☐ I don't have the money.

☐ I hate to fuss.

☐ I hate to put other people to any trouble.

☐ My job comes first—even on my birthday.

☐ Family issues always distract me.

☐ I don't like to think about getting older.

☐ Other _____

_____

Knowing what your barriers are is the first step to overcoming them. We always have the wonderful option of changing our thoughts, and thus our behavior.  Look back at your old thoughts that no longer serve you well. How about writing a new thought that will move you closer to celebrating yourself?

Having breast cancer changed my perspective on birthdays. The more the merrier. I'm happy to be alive!

—Monica S.

age 47

FOR A CHANGE

I love the celebration, but hate being old.

—ELLEN K., AGE 57

For many of the women I've interviewed, the "getting older" issue is often the main celebration obstacle. How about considering a new thought? Each birthday, we will indeed advance one year in age—it's out of our control. It's kind of like Mondays—no matter what our feelings are about this first day of the week, it will still show up. So why not put our energy into what we can control: creating a day that's just the way we'd like it. We're always told, "Pick your battles." That applies to the battles that we fight with ourselves as well.

The other barriers usually revolve around not being a priority in our own lives. As women, we are gold medalists in  this sport. We're always putting ourselves at the bottom of our to-do list. And yet we're unstoppable when it comes to supporting others. Imagine this: A child you love crawls

After the age of sixty, birthdays have become bittersweet . . . but I'll take the bitter with the sweet!

—Kris D.

age 61

into your lap and wants to chat about her upcoming birthday. "What are we going to do to celebrate?" she asks. Would you respond to her with "We won't be celebrating your birthday this year, honey— we just can't seem to squeeze it into our  schedule," or "Sorry, no cupcakes—can't spare the cash." Not a chance. We would never deny a child these simple pleasures, and yet we are so quick to deprive ourselves.

When I started my birthday journal years ago, I pasted a photo of myself in kindergarten on the front page. When I look into her eyes, I wouldn't dream of depriving her of a happy birthday. Do you have a picture of your precious self as a child? Maybe she belongs pasted in the front of this book or in a beautiful frame. She'll always be a reminder to create a celebration that's as special as you are.

YOUR BIRTH-DAY

Your day of birth is the when you started being you! The people you loved and who loved you were never the same again. The world paused for your arrival.

What day were you born?

Do you know what time?

Where?

Did you have any brothers and sisters upon your arrival at home? Who do you suppose was there?

What are some of the best baby stories you've been told about you?

We grew up with barely enough to see us through each day. My mom surprised me when I was turning six and invited six of my friends for cake and ice cream. There were no presents. I know now, this little party was the perfect gift.

—Nikki S.
age 56

WHAT WOULD YOUR BEST FRIEND SAY?

My friend Edie is a career counselor and a general all-around wise woman. She always reminds me that whatever we do naturally in life we tend to take for granted. You operate from your strengths and talents so effortlessly that you neglect to see them as special or unique. You know what I mean: You walk into a friend's house and there's a gorgeous mural painted on the wall and she says, "Oh, it was no big deal—anybody could do it!"

As women, we do the same things to ourselves every day when we undervalue not only our unique skills, but also our natural talents of multitasking, nurturing others, and handling crises. We underestimate the difference we make in our families' lives, at work, in the world. We wake up, breathe, and do what it takes. We forget the spectacular people that we are and how we truly *do* help make the world go round.

Imagine that your best friend is with you now. Ask him or her to name five nice things about you. It's so easy for someone who loves you to respond. Write down what he or she says. (*Your best friend* is doing the talking so no need for modesty!)

1.

2.

3.

4.

5.

Now answer these questions regarding what you've done in just the last week . . .

What tasks have you completed?

Women wear many hats—why not make one of them a crown?

—Lisa C.
age 37

Whose feelings have you soothed?

What traumas and dramas have you faced bravely?

What problems have you solved?

Who feels better because you are you?

Look at both lists and get a load of you! And this is only a tiny piece of the pie—a small slice of who you are naturally and what you're capable of accomplishing. If your friend were reading these lists wouldn't he or she say, "Hon—take a day for yourself—you deserve it!"

The truth is you don't have to do *anything* to deserve your special day. Just being you is enough. You were born. That's worth celebrating. Period.

STEP 2. *It Will Be a Pleasure to Explore My Heart's Desires*

ON THE NEXT few pages you'll find questions that will help you discover and record your heart's desires. These are the ever-so-important pages where you pause and ask yourself, "What do I really enjoy?" You've just been granted time and space to focus on yourself for a moment and become the designer of your birthday, the creator of your happiness.

Every woman's pages will be very different—each of you will have a unique definition of

celebration. "Celebration" is a word that can bring to mind thoughts of hoopla, which may not be what most pleases you. You define what is enjoyable to you by examining your heart's desires, and determining your unique brand of celebrating.

As I have discovered and accepted my own version of the "best celebration," I have also learned to honor others' diverse needs. This took me some time to grasp. I knew that I fit into the "hoopla" category, so I had always assumed that my close friends felt the same way. After all, they were fun, happy people. It was both a loving and an arrogant thought. I discovered just how arrogant when one of my best friends announced, "Linda Marie Sacha, if you love me you will not throw me a surprise party for my fortieth. I despise surprises and I hate being the center of attention. That's YOUR idea of a happy birthday, not mine!"

Busted. My desires are not your desires. I was ready to re-create for her what I loved. It turns out her idea of bliss revolved around margaritas and playing Cranium with five close friends. (Yes, I was invited and we all had a great time doing it *her* way.)

> *A birthday cake is not necessary, and there is never any singing or any other scene at the restaurant. That is how I like it.*
>
> —DEB M., AGE 30

> *On my birthday I try to get other people to spoil me . . . shower me with gifts, buy me dinner, sing. I want attention!*
>
> —LAURA R., AGE 47

After completing my heart's desires pages I realized that I was indeed longing for an "extra cling peach"—AND I wanted to share it! When I looked back at my childhood birthdays, I realized my joy always involved some type of celebration with others. How amazing to discover such an important ingredient that I could use to create happy birthdays for myself. I am finally at peace and no longer feel selfish about the fact that cards and flowers left me feeling like something was missing. Just like when I was a child, share a piece of my peach with me and I'm in birthday heaven.

So what will you discover? On the pages that follow, dare to record your hidden joys and passions. Once these are completed, they will become your template for creating your annual birthday celebration.

HEART'S DESIRES

Initial date of recording: _____

Over the years as you revise or add, use different-colored pens and date your new thoughts. It's fascinating to see how your desires change over time.

Begin by reflecting on your childhood birthdays.

Write about the first birthday of yours that you remember:

Imagine for a moment . . . How do you suppose you felt at your first birthday party?

Record a typical birthday celebration at your house growing up. What did you do? Eat? Who were you with? How did you feel?

Since I was born on Easter Sunday, my mom would make me a bunny cake. It was made with coconut, which I love. The cake was so beautiful that I didn't want to cut it!

— Donna J.
age 54

Did you have a favorite cake?

What was your favorite part of your birthday as a child or one of your sweetest memories?

I like spending my birthday alone, but usually my family
takes me out for a hectic dinner that is not a lot of fun.

—VICKI W., AGE 55

Do you wish it had been different in any way?

Record and reflect on your recent adult birthdays and how they've felt to you:

Sometimes I think the reason my birthday is not a big deal for me is because I like to plan for other people's happiness. I really don't like focusing on myself, but maybe we should, and make ourselves feel good, too.

—KATHY F., AGE 49

How are your childhood and adult birthdays the same? Different?

As a result, what would you like to adjust about your current birthdays?

MY ALL-TIME FAVORITES

I was the sixth of seven children, so money was tight. I remember my mother cooking my favorite meal to celebrate my birthday—fried fish and chocolate pudding.

—INEZ B., AGE 28

What are your favorites?

• **DELECTABLE EDIBLES** •

Home-cooked foods:

Restaurants and specialties:

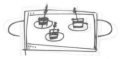

Someone once made me a birthday cake that had little presents wrapped in tinfoil buried between the layers, so that every time you cut a new piece there was a special prize in it! This was pure magic to me. I'm going to make one of those cakes for someone this year.

—Nelie B.

age 47

Desserts:

Special treats:

Favorite kind of birthday "cake" now:

Places to go:

Kinds of entertainment:

My people quotient: privacy, a few friends, a big celebration?

My birthday is a time
when I reflect on my
parents and how thankful
I am to them for having
me and all of the sacrifices
they made.

—Mary S.

age 42

It's not turning forty-nine or fifty that makes birthdays hard, but the attention that I don't like, that people for some false notion think I want.

—SARAH D., AGE 56

Friends and family that I'd like to celebrate with:

• MY DEFINITION OF CELEBRATION •

Birthday "musts":

Birthday "must nots":

What is your "cling peach" (the main ingredient to ensure your birthday joy)?

Thoughts I have about myself and my birthday, after completing these pages:

STEP 3. *I Will Act on My Heart's Desires and Create a Happy Birthday for Myself*

YOU KNOW THAT you deserve a great birthday, and you've uncovered the things you most enjoy—now it's time to create a plan of action. This is where you get to ask yourself, "Am I willing to do what I want for myself and to ask others for what I want?"

When thinking about doing what you want, you might find that the word "selfish" often floats into the picture. This is not about satisfying a selfish whim—rather, it's about meeting a need that is an integral part of who you are. When a plant needs water, you provide it. When the cat is hungry, you feed it. When your friend needs a hug, you hug her. So when you discover what makes your heart sing, why wouldn't you give it what it needs to start singing? Your heart's desires are the very fabric of who you are; of course you want to be sure they are nurtured and met. My friend Vicki put it perfectly: "When I take care of myself, all others are served."

> *My birthday is my day. I don't want to have to remind anyone of it or give any suggestions as to what I want as a gift or celebration.*
>
> —KATHY P., AGE 52

When asking others for what you want, you may have heard yourself say, "If I HAVE to ask, then just forget it." Why would you want to help orchestrate your birthday? So you get what you need and desire! Why should you have to? Well, you don't—as long as you're pleased with how your birthdays have been going. If you would like your birthday to be

I am a miracle, having survived both breast and ovarian cancer. Every day that I wake up is a bonus day. My birthday is a celebration of life . . . MY life.

— Malika S.
age 55

happier, then take the leap and ask for what you want. If you don't speak up, not only is it unfair to yourself, it's unfair to the people in your life who either assume you're happy or wish you were!

Who would you rather hang out with: a woman who walks around smiling because she does what makes her happy and has a full cup for life, or someone who mopes around with an empty cup and wants you to guess how to best fill it up for her? Not only do I want to be friends with the first woman, but I choose to *be* her—I'm certain you do, too.

GUARANTEED

My husband was thrilled when I created a mini-notebook for him called *Guaranteed*. I filled it with info that "guaranteed" my birthday happiness. I included many of the entries from my heart's desires pages and of course, my "cling peach"—a celebration. Then I listed dozens of time-less gifts that I always love getting. I provided names and numbers of the services I enjoy, like dance classes, retreat centers, and massages, along with my clothing sizes and favorite stores. I adore surprises, so I make the list really long so I never know what he's going to choose. There are also general entries like "anything cool for the garden," so that if he's in the mood to get creative, he has flexibility. I never peak in the back of the book because that's where he writes his notes as he notices things that I show interest in throughout the year.

I felt anxious and vulnerable when I presented it to my husband and immediately asked him if he was in-sulted to get a list.

"Insulted?" he replied. "I don't have to guess anymore and have your birthday be something that I dread because I'm sure I'm going to fail. I never knew how important a celebration was to you. I think every woman should do this for her loved ones. I was clueless—why didn't you tell me this stuff sooner?"

Hmmm—why didn't I tell him sooner? Oh, let me list the ways . . .

a) I didn't know it myself.
b) I thought I was telling him through all my years of whining.
c) I didn't know how to ask.
d) I didn't want to sound selfish or demanding.
e) I thought he should just "know."

I celebrate my birthday for seven days.
I tell everyone it's my birthday week!

—Tricia X.

age 53

I feel weird about my birthday, because I haven't cele-brated it in so long that I feel a little guilty and a little indulgent.

—VICKI G., AGE 55

Learning to ask for what you want is a skill that can be acquired. Requests don't have to sound bossy or demanding—here are some examples:

- "Time with you is important; I'd like to meet you for a walk on Tuesday."
- "I was thinking lunch would be fun; I've wanted to try that new place."
- "Birthdays are a big deal to me, so I'd love a phone call from you that day."
- "Will you plan a get-together for me this year? Sur-prise me!"

- "I'd prefer to have a private birthday this year—I've got my own special plans."
- "I could really use some new body lotion."
- "A cake would be great—the whole office can celebrate."
- "Please plan something low-key this year, I'd like to sit back and relax."
- "I'm in the mood to go out and dance!"
- "No need for presents, but I love cards."

What would "guarantee" your happiness this birthday?

What are some great gifts for you that others might not think of without your help?

YOUR DAY YOUR WAY

Here's one of my birthday agendas that I asked for and then arranged. For starters, I took the day off and then several days ahead of time planned the following:

6:00 a.m.	*time alone with my birthday journal*
7:30	*walk and picnic breakfast with girlfriends on the beach*
9:00	*facial and massage—alone!*
12:00 p.m.	*lunch with buddies*
2:30	*shopping with my gift certificate that I asked for from spouse*
5:30	*favorite dinner with hubby at home*
8:00	*meet friends for dessert and music*

As you can see I really packed it in. After years of refining, I've realized that a combination of celebration and private time stretched over a few days gives me the greatest joy. Your agenda will no doubt look different. The point is—YOU examine. YOU choose. YOU orchestrate. YOU enjoy.

. . . .

I take charge of my birthday if no one else does that year. It does not matter whether I plan the fete or someone else does. I know what I want, so why wouldn't I create it for myself?

—Edie D.

age 70

Love yourself enough to put some advance thought into your day. We would never say to a child the morning of her birthday, "So what are you thinking of doing today?" Give yourself that same consideration.

Fill in the following "dream day" birthday agenda:

6:00 a.m.

7:00

8:00

9:00

10:00

11:00

12:00 p.m.

1:00

2:00

3:00

4:00

5:00

6:00

7:00

8:00

9:00

10:00

11:00

THE QUEEN FOR A DAY
"GET TO IT" CHECKLIST

In the last section you examined your heart's desires. For brand-new Birthday Queens who know they want their birthdays to be different from every other day of the year—but aren't quite sure where to begin—my sister Jeanette recommends this nitty-gritty birthday checklist to help you get started.

Put a check mark in all that apply!

For this year's birthday . . .

1. What are you in the mood for?

☐ laughter   ☐ personal growth

☐ contemplation   ☐ outrageousness

☐ learning   ☐ inspiration

☐ privacy   ☐ intimacy

☐ connection   ☐ spiritual food

☐ creative expression   ☐ entertainment

☐ renewal   ☐ accomplishing a dream/goal

2. What ingredients sound appealing?

☐ food   ☐ the arts

☐ the outdoors   ☐ travel

☐ party   ☐ exercise

☐ adventure   ☐ shopping

☐ pampering   ☐ quiet conversation

3. Who do you want to celebrate with?

☐ friends   ☐ family

☐ loved one/partner ☐ myself

☐ strangers   ☐ like-minded people

4. What kind of dress sounds appealing?

☐ comfy   ☐ formal

☐ casual   ☐ dressy

☐ costume   ☐ business

5. How are you going to make it happen?

☐ organize it myself   ☐ discuss it with loved one

☐ call a friend   ☐ check in with family

What ideal birthday picture is emerging?

HOW HAVE OTHER CROWN CARRIERS CELEBRATED?

Since I got married twenty-eight years ago I have planned my own birthdays and told my family what we were doing. A few years ago I decided to make them more exciting for me—so I planned things like hiking, white-water rafting, skiing, and horseback riding.

—MARY J., AGE 54

I like to be with my sisters—shop, talk, eat, and then repeat.

—ROAR R., AGE 33

When I have to work on my birthday, I often don't feel like going out to dinner. However, I still want to be treated to a great meal I didn't have to cook. A wonderful nearby market provides the perfect solution. My husband picks up whatever I want and we enjoy a nice, relax- *ing gourmet dinner at home—complete with dessert and candles. This is more fun than*

When I have a birthday I celebrate for a whole week, which I start out by preparing a luncheon for my lady friends. It's also a time for deep soul-searching, as I realize I must carefully plan these remaining senior years.

— Inge S.
age 75

going out—especially since my birthday is in January and we live in the Northeast!

—ANNA T., AGE 45

The first time I kayaked was at a sixtieth birthday party for me, planned by me.

—EDIE D., AGE 70

I've been on a pretty tight budget, but that never stops me from having fun on my birthday—you just need great friends! I've had celebrations where we had a slumber party, gave one another pedicures, got chick flicks from the library, made dream boards together, each cooked an ingredient for tacos, all brought our baby pictures, visited a senior citizen center with cupcakes—and so much more!

—NINA F., AGE 37

I have started indulging myself with a special treat. This year my friend and I are getting facials and then we are going to see Tina Turner in concert to really celebrate.

—SUE B., AGE 50

On my birthday I buy new makeup and update my look.

—LEILANI P., AGE 42

STEP 4. *I Accept Responsibility for My Birthday: I Own It*

WHETHER YOU LOVED your last birthday or it was less than perfect, make sure to give yourself the credit either way. One year you may have a day that's peaches and another may be the pits. As long as we take responsibility for our day, we are still claiming our crown. If your birthday was lousy, look at what contributed to the lousiness, and do it differently next year. If it was fabulous, celebrate how you contributed to its fabulousness. Either way—own it!

Why own it? Because we are not victims—

we have the amazing ability to continually look at how we contribute to both our successes and our less-than-successful life events. I have found that some years do indeed require greater flexibility and creativity than others. When the kids are little, parents are sick, or careers are demanding, we adjust, but we don't give up completely. We get to ask ourselves, "How can I still make this a special day for myself?

What is one small thing that will fulfill a piece of my heart's desire?" Some years it may be as simple as a warm bath. As long as you are willing to accept your own choices, you're in charge of your own joy.

We evacuated for Hurricane Floyd and got home the day before my fortieth birthday. No one called to say happy birthday because they were all being hammered by the hurricane. My husband pulled a family dinner together at our house and called me at four p.m. to ask me if I could vacuum! I know my forty-first will be better!

—SUE B., AGE 40

A few years ago my birthday was looking a bit shaky—I was seriously considering ditching my birthday commitment. My husband was wildly sick with the flu, my sisters were across the country, my parents were celebrating in heaven, and we'd moved many states away from all my cronies. I got cards. I got calls. I got a couple of e-mails. Shouldn't that be enough? "This birthday is just going to be different," I heard the old familiar voice chime in. I took a deep breath. Okay, several deep breaths. Was I willing to settle and abandon my heart's desires? How could I salvage this birthday and create the celebration I love in some small way? The queen in me adjusted her crown. This year is different, yes—hopeless, NO!

I ventured out into the snow to a new deli and chose a beautiful meal to go. As I perused the dessert counter I couldn't believe my eyes. There before me was my all-time favorite childhood delight: homemade, not instant, butterscotch pudding. It had been twenty years and there it was, the dessert special of the day! I came home, warmed my dinner, put a candle  in my pudding, poured my husband some ginger ale, and asked him to

Hail to the Birthday Queen!
The journey to rediscovering
a happy birthday has been
challenging AND totally
worth it because I discovered
that I'm totally worth it.

Molly F.

age 54

sing with me. I was thrilled that I had carved out a slice of joy for myself on a less-than-perfect day.

He was thrilled by my willingness to take charge of my own happiness when he was sick and feeling so helpless.

That was a close call and a true test of my commitment to my birthday happiness and myself. There will continue to be additional growth opportunities, but each time the learning comes more quickly and it's a lot more satisfying.

So accept all the credit you deserve if you've created a day that's worth remembering—one way or another. Accept. Adjust. Grow.

> *You asked me if I was pleased with my birthdays, and when I think about an answer of no, I'm reminded of the story about the man who complains every day about his homemade lunch. Finally after hearing enough of his complaining, his friend asked him, "Why don't you ask your wife to fix you something else for lunch?" The man replied, "Oh, my wife doesn't fix my lunch. I do." We get in life exactly what we choose! So if I am not pleased with my birthday, I know who gets to change it!*
>
> —LINDA S., AGE 52

Can you recall a birthday that was less than memorable? What happened?

How can you use the lessons learned from that birthday to shape future birthdays?

STEP 5. *In an Annual Loving Birthday Ritual, I Will Capture My Thoughts, Feelings, and Dreams*

EACH YEAR WHEN January 1st arrives, there are celebrations, declarations, and resolutions. The entire world has claimed this holiday. Why not create your own personal New Year on your day of birth? It's got all the right ingredients: It happens every year, you'll be there, it's clearly a time of celebration, and it's all yours! It's an annual opportunity to assess your life and reinvent yourself.

The annual birthday journal invites you to

reflect on and celebrate the past months and  dream about the upcoming year. I love going back and reading my past entries; it's amazing how our lives and priorities shift as we grow. It's even more amazing to feel and live the effects of it all.

It's all about you. How can you go wrong?

> *My birthday is a day I try to do some reflection about my life and where I am. How has the last year been? What significant accomplishments have I completed and what am I planning for next year?*
>
> —LEILANI P., AGE 42

PART 3

Your Annual Birthday Journal

Happy Birthday!

Date: _____

Welcome to your crowning initiation. Long may you reign!

This is time just for you . . .

Have you planned for no interruptions?

How about your favorite music?

Are you comfy and in a peaceful location?

HIGHLIGHTS

My accomplishments that felt "big":

Three other valuable accomplishments:

1.

2.

3.

The biggest challenges that I faced:

Three qualities and talents I used to tackle my accomplishments and challenges:

1.

2.

3.

My birthday is very important to me, and even more so
with every passing year. Each
year there is more to celebrate,
whether a child's marriage, a
new grandchild, new friends,
old friends, another year on
this earth.

—Suzanne D.
age 70

This year I discovered:

A nice compliment I received:

Over the past year I have grown personally in the following ways:

I have grown professionally in the following ways:

I visited new places:

I met new people:

Three things I am especially grateful for:

1.

2.

3.

THE "NEW YEAR"

I like to put up on a big board what I see for myself for the next year. I review the year gone by, which then leads me to create my vision for the year to come.

—JILL B., AGE 62

This year I want more:

This year I want less:

Three things I intend to accomplish:

1.

2.

3.

My professional goals for this year include:

Over this year I hope for my family life to grow in the following ways:

My hopes for my social life this year include:

In the coming year I hope to improve my relationship
with the following people:

I'm interested in learning more about:

I intend to make more time for:

I am really looking forward to:

At this time next year I hope to be:

On this date five years from now I see myself:

CELEBRATION

*My fiftieth was my favorite birthday! I made a point of
seeing everyone I loved most and celebrating their pres-
ence in my life.*

—LORE G., AGE 52

Read page 28, "Queen for a Day Credo." Journal your thoughts
and feelings on which statements feel comfortable and which
are currently growth opportunities.

What are your birthday plans for this year—and if you've already done them, how did they go?

How are you considering your heart's desires on page 54 or the "Get to It" Checklist on page 81?

Photos, sketches, or other birthday memorabilia:

Now you have the opportunity to buy yourself the perfect birthday journal for all of your birthdays to come. Do you want it this size? Would you prefer a big artist's pad? A small secret diary with a lock? Create a "day away" for yourself and go on a search for the perfect book that will hold all of your future celebrations.

Of course, it must be as unique as you.

ACKNOWLEDGMENTS

Please put on your party hat and help me give a hand to . . .

The one and only Birthday Board of Directors—Molly Lord, Roar Rowley, Deborah Prater, Anna Maria Trusky, and Nikki Sweet. Thank you, thank you, thank you for who and how you are.

Karen Gerwin from The Creative Culture. Brianne Mulligan and the team at Gotham Books. Thank you for your immense guidance and kindness in helping the princess mature.

Women from around the world who bravely shared their birthday pains and pleasures with me.

John Sacha, my husband, best friend, and prince—you are a dream come true.

And to Steffanie Ziev who escorted the Queen.

ABOUT THE AUTHOR

Linda M. Sacha celebrated her childhood birthdays outside Buffalo, New York. A woman on a lifelong quest to know, love, and trust herself fully, Sacha is fiercely committed to supporting others on the same path. She enjoys a multifaceted career as a life support coach, writer and an award-winning speaker and voice-over artist. A recovered birthday pouter, Sacha lives in Florida with her prince and their rescue Chihuahua.

Please visit www.lindasacha.com